# MY PET

# Puppy

Honor Head

Photographs by Jane Burton

Belitha Press

First published in the UK in 2000 by
Belitha Press
An imprint of Chrysalis Books plc
64 Brewery Road, London N7 9NT

Paperback edition first published in 2002

ISBN 1 84138 084 9 (hardback)
ISBN 1 84138 356 2 (paperback)

British Library Cataloguing in
Publication Data for this book is
available from the British Library.

Editor: Claire Edwards
Designer: Rosamund Saunders
Illustrator: Pauline Bayne
Consultant: Frazer Swift

Printed in Hong Kong

10 9 8 7 6 5 4 3 2 1

**Some dogs in this book are shown without collars. This is for photographic purposes only.**

PDSA (People's Dispensary for Sick Animals) is Britain's largest charity which each year provides free treatment for some 1.4 million sick and injured animals of disadvantaged owners.

A royalty of 2.5 per cent of the proceeds from this book will be paid to the PDSA (People's Dispensary for Sick Animals) on every copy sold in the UK.

The products featured have been kindly donated by Pets at Home.

# Contents

# My puppy

coat

claws

paws

# It's fun owning your own pet.

Puppies look sweet and are fun
to play with, but they need
to be looked after carefully.

A puppy needs feeding
every day and
grooming regularly.
It will also have to be
trained. Most of all,
remember that your
puppy will grow up
and be with you for
a long time.

Young children with
pets should always
be supervised
by an adult. For
further notes, please
see page 32.

# Dogs come in all shapes and sizes.

Small dogs can be easier to look after than large dogs. They need less space at home and eat less. But they still need plenty of exercise and attention.

This collie, border terrier and smooth-haired dachshund will all make lovely pets but each breed has its own special needs.

Big dogs can be very strong and need long walks each day. They can be rough when they play and could knock you over.

Purebred dogs like this one can be very expensive to buy. Mongrel dogs are a mixture of lots of breeds.

# A pregnant bitch needs extra care.

A female dog is called a
bitch. When she is pregnant
her tummy grows bigger as
the puppies grow. You can
see the puppies moving inside
her. A mother dog needs
treating very gently.

When a bitch becomes
pregnant her shape
changes. Her
stomach grows
bigger and rounder.

The pregnant mother will look for a cosy, quiet place to have her puppies. A box or basket lined with newspaper and blankets is ideal for her.

You can watch the puppies being born, but do not go too near.

A mother usually has between four and eight puppies, but she may have more. The new puppies can only just crawl.

# When puppies are born, they can't see or hear.

Puppies are born with their eyes and ears closed. They find their way to their mother's milk by smell. Drinking her milk is called suckling.

As the puppies grow older they will jump all over each other. They squeal and yelp but they are only playing.

These puppies are one day old. While they are asleep, the mother can stretch her legs and have something to eat.

Puppies need to be wormed and see the vet when they are about four weeks old.

The mother licks her puppies to keep them clean. They can be gently stroked now.

# Soon the puppies will be old enough to leave their mother.

When a puppy is about eight weeks old it is old enough to leave its mother. It may be frightened and miss its family. When you take a puppy home, talk to it quietly so that it gets to know your voice.

Puppies sleep a lot. Don't wake a puppy when it is asleep. When it is tired of playing, let it rest.

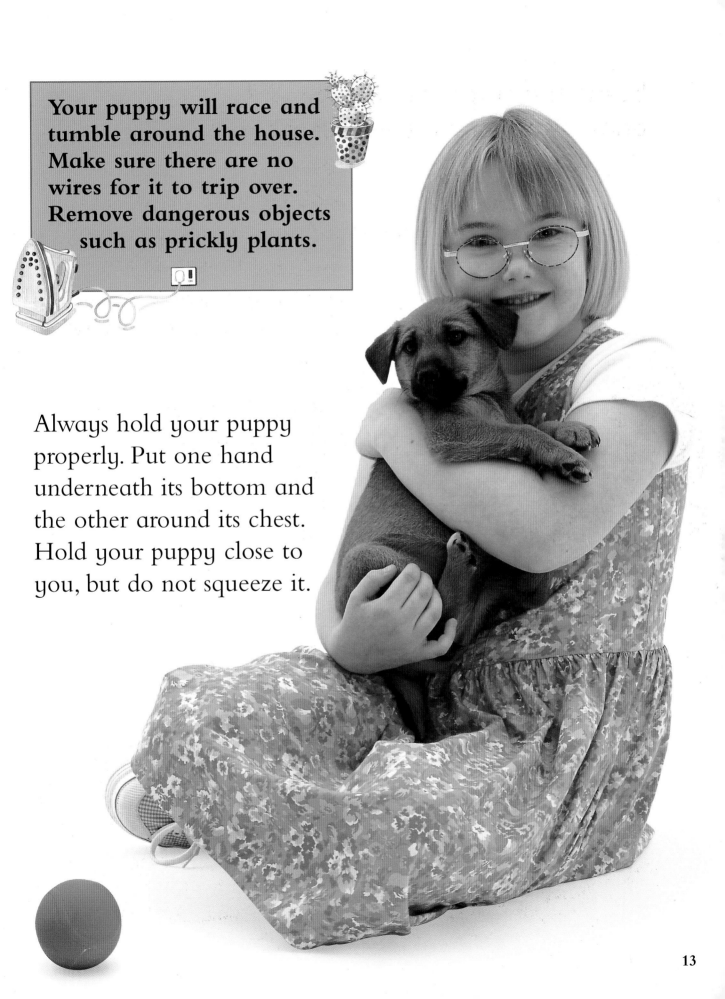

Your puppy will race and tumble around the house. Make sure there are no wires for it to trip over. Remove dangerous objects such as prickly plants.

Always hold your puppy properly. Put one hand underneath its bottom and the other around its chest. Hold your puppy close to you, but do not squeeze it.

# Puppies enjoy playing.

Puppies often pretend to fight each other. They are just playing and won't hurt each other.

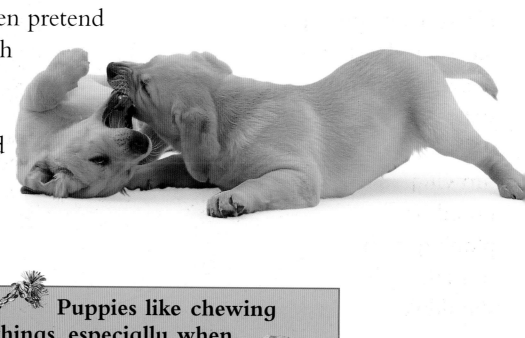

Puppies like chewing things, especially when their teeth are growing.

You can play games with your puppy. Throw a ball for it to catch, or play tug of war gently with a piece of cloth. If your puppy bites you playfully, say 'no' in a firm voice.

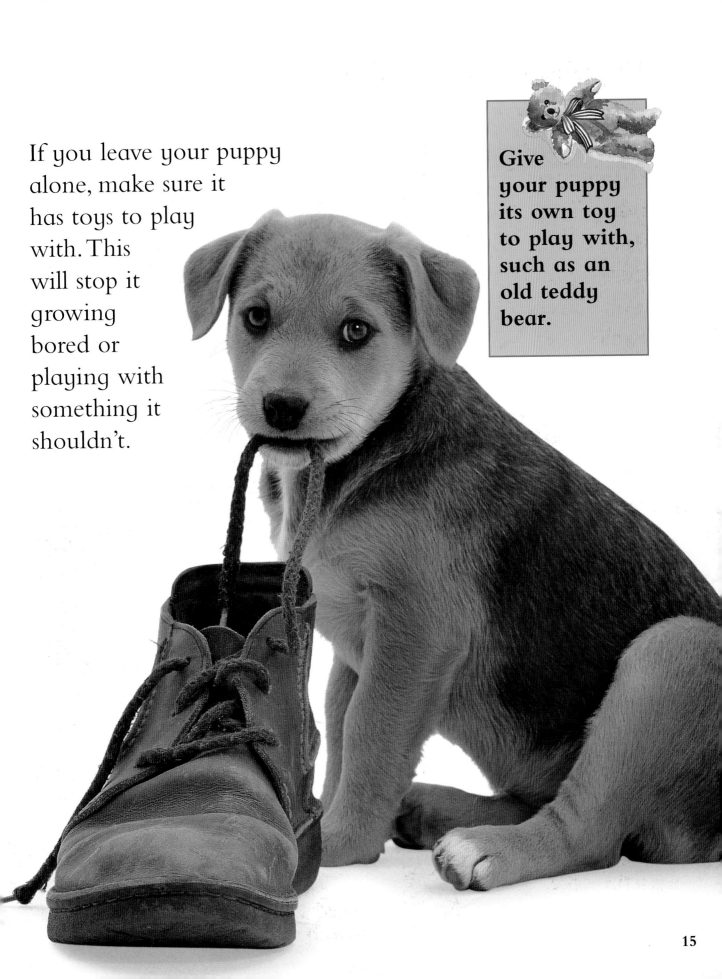

If you leave your puppy alone, make sure it has toys to play with. This will stop it growing bored or playing with something it shouldn't.

Give your puppy its own toy to play with, such as an old teddy bear.

# Make your puppy feel at home.

Find somewhere quiet
and warm for your
puppy's bed. You can
buy a basket from
a pet shop or make
one yourself. Put
a blanket inside.

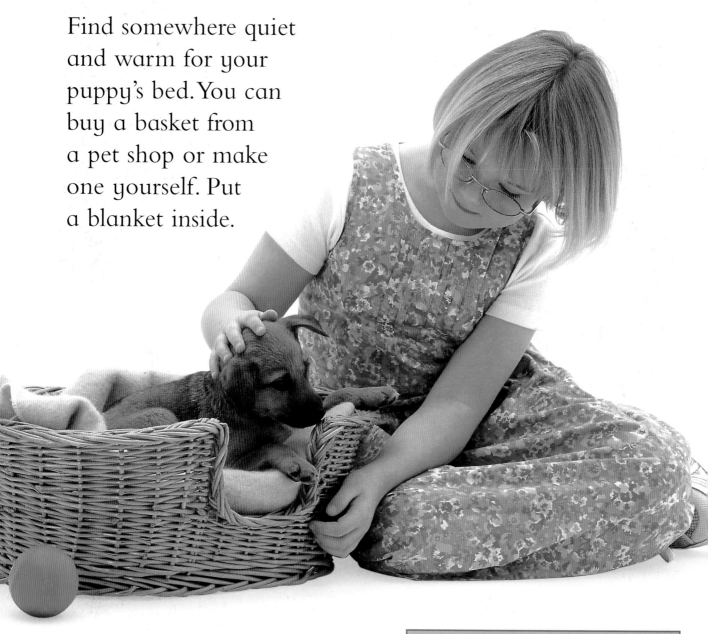

To make a bed for
your dog, cut the
front from a box
and line it with
a warm blanket.

Buy special bowls for your puppy – one for food and one for water. Feed it small meals four times a day. Make sure it always has fresh water to drink.

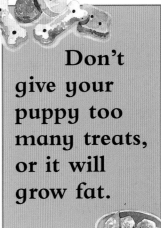

**Don't give your puppy too many treats, or it will grow fat.**

Your puppy will enjoy bone-shaped chews. These will help to keep its teeth clean and strong. Do not give your puppy cooked or small bones as these can make it choke. Buy large, uncooked marrow bones from the butcher.

# You will need to train your puppy.

Once your puppy has settled in, teach it its name. Stand or sit a little way away and call its name. When it comes to you give it a big hug.

When you feed or play with your puppy, say its name so that it grows used to hearing it.

Your puppy must learn to sit when it is told to do so. Each time your puppy sits, say the word 'sit'. Make a fuss of your puppy when it does as you ask.

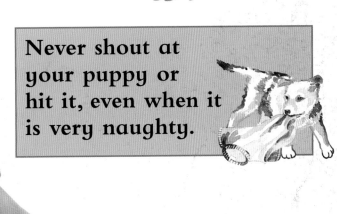

Your puppy must be toilet trained. Take it outside after it has eaten, before bed and when it wakes up. If it sniffs about and looks as if it is going to make a mess, call a grown-up.

# Take your puppy to see the vet.

When your puppy is about 12 weeks old, you should to take it to the vet. Take it on the lead or in a special dog carrier.

Your vet will tell you when your puppy is old enough to be neutered. This is an operation to prevent unwanted puppies.

The vet will give your puppy a general check-up and some injections. She will look at its ears and teeth to make sure your puppy is healthy.

If your puppy is unwell, make sure it is kept warm and in a quiet place.

If your puppy has an upset stomach, is very quiet and doesn't eat, it may need to visit the vet. If your puppy is ill, treat it gently. Make sure it has a bowl of fresh water to drink.

# Your puppy needs a walk every day.

You should not let your puppy meet other dogs until it has had all its injections. When your puppy is used to its lead, take it for a walk. Do not pull your puppy by the lead.

All dogs must wear a collar and tag with the owner's name and telephone number on it.

Train your puppy to walk by your side. If it tugs on the lead, say 'heel'. If it still tugs, say, 'sit'. Praise it when it does the right thing.

**If your dog goes to the toilet, use a scoop and a plastic bag to clear up the mess.**

If you are near farm animals or close to a road, always keep your puppy on the lead. Train it to sit by your side before you cross the road.

# Keep your puppy clean.

When you come back from a walk in the rain, or through a muddy field or park, wipe your dog with a towel to keep it clean and dry.

Your puppy will learn to clean itself, but you should brush it for a few minutes every day to help keep its coat healthy. This is called grooming.

**Buy a special brush and comb to groom your puppy. Brush the coat gently from the head down to the tail.**

If your puppy keeps scratching, it might have fleas. These insects live in its fur. Ask your vet for some flea spray or powder.

# How is your puppy feeling?

When your puppy runs to you with its tail in the air and its ears pointed up it is happy.

Your puppy may sit up and look at you with its head on one side. This means it is hoping for a game or a treat.

When a puppy is unhappy or scared it keeps its head down or tucks its tail between its legs. It might need a big hug.

When your puppy crouches with its bottom in the air, it wants to play. It may also wag its tail from side to side.

If a puppy is angry, it crouches down, growls and shows its teeth. If your puppy looks like this, leave it alone.

# Your puppy will soon grow up.

By the time your puppy is about
a year old it will be a fully grown
dog. Big dogs change a lot as they
grow, but smaller dogs do not
look very different.

As your dog grows older it will
sleep more and play less. It will
still enjoy being hugged, stroked
and brushed.

Dogs live for 18 years or more, but like people they grow old and die. If your pet is very ill or badly injured, it may also die.

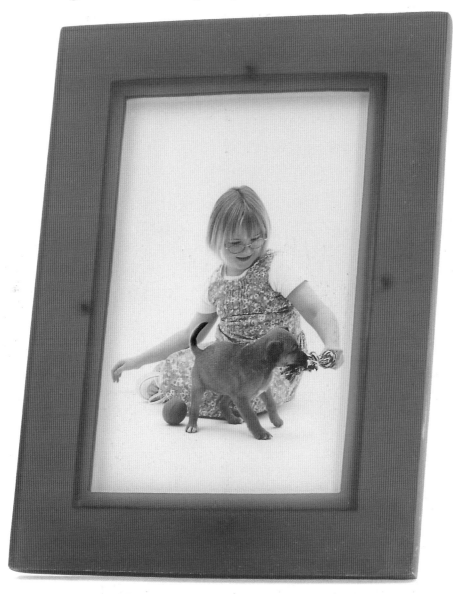

You may feel sad when this happens but you will be able to look back and remember all the happy times you had together.

# Words to remember

**bitch** A female dog.

**breed** A type of dog.

**chews** Treats made specially for dogs.

**coat** A dog's fur.

**fleas** Tiny, biting insects that live in a dog's fur.

**groom** To brush or comb your dog's coat.

**growl** The noise a dog makes when it is angry or scared. It makes the noise with its mouth closed.

**mongrel** A dog that is a mixture of several breeds.

**purebred** A dog that has been specially bred from other dogs of the same breed.

**suckling** When a puppy drinks its mother's milk it is suckling.

**treats** Special snacks.

**vet** An animal doctor.

**wormed** Treated by the vet to stop an animal having worms. These could live in its stomach and make it ill.

**A newborn puppy.**

**At three weeks a puppy likes to sleep a lot.**

**At eight weeks a puppy is old enough to leave its mother.**

# Index

# Notes for parents

A dog will give you and your family a great deal of pleasure, but it is a big responsibility. If you decide to buy a puppy for your child, you will need to ensure that the animal is healthy, happy and safe. You will have to train and feed your pet, and care for it if it is ill. You will also have to supervise your child with the animal until he or she is at least five years old.

Here are some other points to think about before you decide to own a dog:

- A dog can live for about 18 years and can cost a lot of money in food and vet's bills. A dog needs an annual injection and regular worming. An average-sized dog can cost more than £700 a year to look after.

- If you go out to work, do not leave your dog on its own all day. If you have holidays abroad, you will have to pay kennels fees.

- All male and female dogs should be neutered to prevent unwanted litters.

Different breeds of dogs have different temperaments. Some are more excitable than others, so choose your breed carefully. A vet will be able to advise you on which breed is suitable for you:

- Do you have very young or elderly people in the house?

- How often and for how long can you take your dog walking?

- Do you have a garden? Is there a park or open space nearby?

All dogs by law should have a collar and identification tag. Vets can now insert a tiny microchip, the size of a grain of rice, under the dog's skin. This can be scanned to give details of the dog's owners.

This book is intended as an introduction only for young readers. If you have any queries about how to look after your puppy, you can contact the PDSA (People's Dispensary for Sick Animals) at Whitechapel Way, Priorslee, Telford, Shropshire TF2 9PQ. Tel: 01952 290999.